Oxford Progressive Englis~
General Editor: D.H. ~

Two Boxes of Gold and O~

... *Easter Readers* series provides a
wide ran~ ... learners of English. It includes
... ies of young readers, and also
modern fiction ... readers: the *Introductory*
Grade at a 1400-word level, *Grade 1* at a 2100 word level,
Grade 2 at a 2100 word level, *Grade 3* at a 2700 word level
and *Grade 4* which consists of abridged works. Structural
as well as lexical controls are applied at each level.

Wherever possible the mood and style of the original
stories have been retained. Where this requires departure
from the grading scheme, definitions and notes are given.

All the books in the series are attractively illustrated.
Each book als~ ... short section containing questions and
suggested acti~...

Two Boxes of Gold and Other Stories

Charles Dickens

Hong Kong
OXFORD UNIVERSITY PRESS
Oxford Singapore Tokyo

Oxford University Press

Oxford New York Toronto
Kuala Lumpur Singapore Hong Kong Tokyo
Delhi Bombay Calcutta Madras Karachi
Nairobi Dar es Salaam Cape Town
Melbourne Auckland

and associated companies in
Beirut Berlin Ibadan Mexico City Nicosia

© Oxford University Press 1979
First published 1979
Fifth impression 1985

OXFORD is a trade mark of Oxford University Press

Retold by Jean Oxley
Illustrated by Rosemary Parsons
Cover illustration by Monica May
Simplified according to the language grading scheme
especially compiled by D.H. Howe

ISBN 0 19 581212 3

Printed in Hong Kong by Winson Printing Co.
Published by Oxford University Press, Warwick House, Hong Kong

Contents

Contents

1 Black Coll and the Devil's Inn

This is the story of a house called the Devil's Inn. It stands
in a small valley in the Connemara mountains in Ireland. It
was built by a stranger. No one knew where he had come
from, and the people living near gave him the name Black
Coll. They called his house the Devil's Inn. No one had ever   5
been known to enter the house as a friend, and Black Coll
lived alone except for an old servant. They were an unpleasant
pair.

During the first year that they lived in the valley, there had
been many guesses as to who they were. Some said that Black   10
Coll was a member of the family who had owned land round
about. They thought he had come to try and get his land
back. Others said he had done something very wrong, and
thought he might have run away from another country. Some
whispered that he had been cursed at birth, and could not   15
smile or make friends with anyone till the day he died. But
no one really knew anything about the two men, and when
two years had passed, the people began to forget that they
were there.

The years passed until one day news came that Colonel   20
Blake, the new landowner, was coming to visit the country.
By climbing one of the mountains near his home, Black Coll
could look down and see an old house. It had been empty for
many years, but now workmen were repairing the walls and
windows. Other men were busy painting fences. He watched   25
them for several months, but never went down to see the
house when they had finished it.

It was autumn when Colonel Blake, his only daughter, and
a party of friends came to the house. Now the house was full
of life and laughter, but Black Coll was no longer interested   30
in watching it from his mountain top. He kept away from the
house, and from the people who were living there.

One evening in September the wind changed, and in half an hour the mountains were covered in thick cloud. Black Coll was far from his home, but he knew the mountain paths so well that he was not frightened by storms, rain or thick clouds. But while he was walking along he heard a cry. He quickly followed the sound, and came to a man who was completely lost and in danger of death at every step.

'Follow me,' said Black Coll to this man. In an hour he had brought him safely down to the house he had watched for so many months.

The Colonel's daughter

'I am Colonel Blake,' said the man when they at last stood in the starlight under the lighted windows of the house. 'Please tell me quickly to whom I owe my life.'

'Colonel Blake,' said Black Coll, after a strange silence, 'your father made my father lose all his money and lands at a game of cards. Both are dead, but you and I live, and I have promised myself that I will kill you.'

The Colonel laughed at Black Coll's unhappy face.

'And you began to keep your promise tonight by saving my life,' he said. 'Come, I am a soldier, and I know how to meet an enemy. But I would far rather meet a friend. I shall not be happy until you have eaten a meal with us. It is my daughter's birthday, please come in and join us.'

Black Coll looked down at the ground.

'I have told you who and what I am,' he said, 'and I will not come into your house.'

At that moment a door opened near them and a girl appeared. She was quite tall and dressed in white silk. Her face was as pale as her dress. There were pearls around her throat, and red roses in her hair. Black Coll had never seen anything more beautiful.

Evleen Blake went up to her father.

'Thank God you are safe,' she said. 'The others have been home for an hour.'

'My dear, I owe my life to this brave gentleman,' said the Colonel. 'Try to make him come in and be our guest. He wants to return to the mountains and lose himself again in the clouds where I found him, or rather where he found me.'

'I beg you to come in, sir,' said Evleen. 'If you had not found my father, this night of happiness would have been turned into sorrow.' She held out her hand to the tall man. He took it and held it tightly. The proud girl's eyes flashed with surprise, for his strength had hurt her. Was this Black Coll mad, or rude?

The guest no longer refused to enter, and followed the girl into a little room where a lamp was burning. Now they could all see clearly. Evleen looked at the stranger's dark face, and felt great fear and dislike.

So Black Coll was present at Evleen Blake's birthday party. Here he was, under a roof that should have been his own. Here he was, having waited for years for the chance to kill the man who had been the cause of so much unhappiness. His mother had died of a broken heart, his father had killed himself, his brothers and sisters had all gone away. Here he stood, like Samson without his strength, all because of this lovely girl who looked so beautiful in white silk and red roses.

One red rose

Evleen moved among her guests, trying not to notice those strange eyes which followed her wherever she went. Her father asked her to be kind to the man who had saved his life. She took him to see the new picture gallery, and explained the paintings to him. She showed him many works of art, trying to move his attention from herself. But it did not matter what she said, he still kept his eyes on her. They stopped for a moment by an open window. Through it there was a view over the sea. The full moon was high in the sky.

'My father planned this window himself,' said the girl. 'Don't you think it is well done?'

Black Coll did not reply to her question, but suddenly

asked her for a rose from a bunch of flowers pinned to the
front of her dress.

For the second time that night Evleen Blake's eyes flashed
in angry surprise. But this man had saved her father's life. She
broke off a flower and held it out to him. He took the rose,
and also the hand that gave it, and covered it with kisses.

'Sir,' she cried angrily, 'if you are a gentleman you must be
mad. If you are not mad, then you are not a gentleman.'

'Be kind,' said Black Coll, 'I love you. I have never loved a
woman before. Ah,' he cried, as a look of dislike crept over
her face, 'you hate me. You were afraid the first time your
eyes met mine. I love you, and you hate me.'

'I do,' cried Evleen. 'Please, don't talk like this again.'

'I won't trouble you any longer,' said Black Coll. And
walking to the window, he placed one strong hand on the
edge, and jumped out of her sight.

The Burrag-bos

All through that night Black Coll walked in the mountains,
but not towards his own home. He had not eaten since the
morning before, and at sunrise was glad to see a small house.
He walked in and asked for water to drink and a place where
he might rest.

There had been a death in the house, and the kitchen was
full of people. They had come to watch over the body all
night and to pray. Many were asleep, but those who were
awake crossed themselves when they heard Black Coll's evil
name. But an old man invited him in and gave him some
milk, promising some food later. He took him to a small
room off the kitchen. In the room were two women sitting
by the fire, and at one end a small bed.

'A traveller,' said the old man to the two women, and they
nodded their heads. Black Coll went to the bed and lay
down.

The women stopped talking for a while, but when they
thought that the visitor was asleep they began again. There

was only a tiny window in the room, but Black Coll could see
the two women in the light of the fire. One was very old, the
other quite a young girl.

'It's the funniest marriage I ever heard of,' the girl said.
'Only three weeks ago, he was telling everyone that he hated   *5*
her like poison.'

'I know,' said the old woman, 'but what could he do, poor
man, when she put the Burrag-bos on him?'

'The what?' asked the girl.

'The Burrag-bos, my dear. It's a magic charm.'   *10*

'But what is it?' asked the girl, eagerly. 'What's the Burrag-
bos, and where did she get it?'

'I shouldn't tell you, you're too young, but listen. It's a
strip of the skin of a dead body. It must be taken from the
top of the head to the heel without a crack or a break, or the   *15*
charm is broken. Then it is rolled up and put on a piece of
string round the neck of the one you want to love you. It
works very quickly.'

The girl was looking at her friend in horror.

'How terrible,' she cried. 'No one on earth would dare to   *20*
do such an awful, bad thing.'

'Well, there is one person who does it, and that's Pexie.
Haven't you ever heard of her?'

The girl nodded. 'She lives up in the hills,' she whispered.

'Well, she will do it for money any day. They hunted her   *25*
from the graveyard at Salruck, where she had raised the dead.
They would have killed her, but they couldn't find her afterwards.'

'Hush,' whispered the girl, 'the traveller is getting up. What
a short rest he has had.'   *30*

It was enough for Black Coll, however. He had got up, and
now made his way back to the kitchen. The old man was
there, and had some food ready for the traveller. When he
had eaten, Black Coll set off for the mountains again, just as
the sun was rising. By sunset he was walking in the hills   *35*
looking for Pexie's house.

The witch

He found her at last in a tiny broken-down hut. She was an ugly old woman, dressed in a red blanket. Her black hair stuck out from under an orange scarf which was tied round her head. She was bending over a pot upon her fire, and she
5 gave Black Coll an evil look as he came near.

He told her what he wanted.

'Ah, the Burrag-bos. But I'll want some money. The Burrag-bos is hard to get.'

'I will pay,' said Black Coll, and he put some money down
10 on her table.

The old witch fell on it, and laughing, she gave her visitor a look which made even Black Coll feel frightened.

'You're a fine man,' she said, 'and I will get you the Burrag-bos. But the money is not enough. More, more.'
15 She stretched out her claw-like hand, and Black Coll dropped some more money into it. She screamed with happiness.

'Now, listen to me,' said Black Coll. 'I have paid you well, but if your devil's charm does not work, I will have you
20 hunted down and killed as a witch.'

'Work,' cried Pexie, rolling up her eyes. 'Of course it will work. Even if she hates you now, she will love you like her own soul before the sun sets or rises. That, or the girl will go mad before one hour is up.'
25 'You made that last part up,' cried Black Coll. 'I heard nothing of madness. If you want more money, say so, but don't try any of your evil tricks on me.'

The witch fixed her evil eyes on him.

'You guessed the truth,' she said, 'it is only a little more
30 money poor Pexie wants.'

Again the claw-like hand was held out. Black Coll would not touch it, but threw the money on the table.

'When shall I get it?' he asked.

'You must come back here in twelve days, for the Burrag-
35 bos is hard to get. The lonely graveyard is far away, and the

dead man is hard to raise . . .'

'Silence,' cried Black Coll, 'not a word more. I will have
your terrible charm, but what it is, and where you get it, I
will not know.'

Then, promising to come back in twelve days, he went   5
away.

In twelve days Black Coll got the promised charm. He
sewed it into a cloth of gold, and put it on a fine chain. Then
he put it into a box. It looked very pretty.

However, while he was doing this, the people of the moun-   10
tains were angry. There had been another unholy act in their
graveyard, and they were planning to find the person who
had done it.

An evil plan

Two weeks passed. How could Black Coll find the chance
to put the charm around the neck of the Colonel's daughter?   15
More money was dropped into Pexie's greedy hand, and then
she agreed to help him.

Next morning the witch dressed herself in better clothes.
She did her black hair under a snow-white cap, and by magic,
made herself look younger. Then she went out into the hills   20
to gather mushrooms. The housekeeper at the Colonel's
house bought mushrooms from her every morning. Every
morning she left a bunch of flowers for Miss Evleen Blake,
saying that she had never seen her, but had heard that she
was so pretty.   25

At last she met Miss Evleen one morning. She went up to
her and gave her the flowers herself.

'Ah,' said Evleen, 'it is you who leave me flowers every
morning. They are very sweet.'

Yes, Pexie had wanted to see if what she had heard was   30
true. And now she had seen her beautiful face she would go
away. Yet she waited a while.

'Has my lady ever been up into the big mountains?' asked
Pexie.

'No,' replied Evleen, laughing. She was sure she could not walk up a mountain.

'Oh, but you should go,' said Pexie. 'Go with your friends, and ride on pretty little donkeys. There are many beautiful things for you to see up in the mountains.'

She told Evleen such wonderful stories about the mountains that Evleen began to think that she must make the trip.

Not long after this Black Coll received a message from Pexie. She told him that a group of people from the big house would go into the mountains the next day. Evleen Blake would be with them. Black Coll must be ready to feed a crowd of tired and hungry people, who in the evening would be brought to his door. Muireade, the mushroom seller, would meet the group up in the mountains, and would offer to act as their guide. She would lead them far out of their way, up steep slopes and across dangerous places. To escape from these, she would tell the servants to throw away the baskets of food which they carried.

Black Coll was very busy. He managed, probably by black magic, to prepare a great feast for his expected guests. His empty rooms suddenly became full of beautiful furniture and pictures. Servants appeared from nowhere, and stood ready to carry in the wonderful food.

At last, the tired party came in sight of Black Coll's house, the Devil's Inn, and Black Coll went out to invite them inside. Colonel Blake was very pleased to see him. Evleen had not told her father about Black Coll's strange behaviour towards her.

Everyone went into the feast except for Evleen Blake. She stayed outside the door. She was tired, but did not want to rest there. She was hungry, but unwilling to eat Black Coll's food. Black Coll and the Colonel came to the door and begged her to enter, the servants brought her food, but she would not go in, and she would not eat.

'Poison, poison,' she whispered, and threw the food away.

But it was different when Pexie, the kindly old woman, the mushroom seller with all the wicked lines smoothed out of her face, came to the door. She brought a dish of cooked mushrooms to Evleen.

'Ah, my lady,' she said, 'I have cooked these just for you.'

Then Evleen took the plate and ate all the mushrooms. She had hardly finished when she began to feel very sleepy, and *5* she sat down on the door-step. She put her head against the side of the door, and was soon fast asleep.

'Silly girl,' said the Colonel when he found her. He picked her up and carried her into one of the rooms. It had been empty that morning, but now contained a beautiful bed, *10* covered in rich material. The Colonel laid his daughter on the bed and took his last look at her lovely face.

The charm works

The Colonel went back to his friends, and soon after, the whole group went out to watch the beautiful sunset. Black Coll went with them, but when they had gone some distance, *15* he remembered he had to go back and fetch something. He was not away long, but he was away long enough to go into the room where Evleen was still sleeping and throw a light chain round her neck. The Burrag-bos slipped among the folds of her dress. *20*

After he had gone, Pexie crept to the door. She opened it a little, and sat down on a mat outside. An hour passed, and Evleen Blake still slept. Her breathing hardly moved the awful thing that lay on her breast. After that she began to moan, and Pexie knew she was waking up. Soon, a sound in *25* the room told her that the girl was awake and had got up. Pexie put her face to the open door and looked in. She gave a scream of fear, and ran from the house, and was never seen in that country again.

It was nearly dark now, and the walkers were returning *30* towards the Devil's Inn. A group of ladies, who were far ahead of the rest, met Evleen Blake. She came towards them and they noticed something bright, like gold, hanging round her neck. They went to talk to her, but she stared at them in

a strange way, and passed on. They thought she was very rude to behave like that, and went on their way.

Evleen ran on. A rabbit crossed her path and she laughed loudly. Clapping her hands she ran after it. Then she stopped and talked to the stones, hitting them with her hand when   5 they did not answer her. Soon she began to call after the birds in a wild voice. Some of the gentlemen, returning by a dangerous path, heard the noise and stopped to listen.

'What's that?' asked one.

'A young eagle,' said Black Coll, 'they often cry like that.'   10

'It was very much like a woman's voice,' said another. As he spoke another wild sound rang out from the rocks above. There was a piece of rock sticking out over a steep drop to the valley below. As they watched, they saw Evleen Blake moving towards this dangerous place.   15

'My Evleen,' cried the Colonel. 'She is mad to walk in such a dangerous place.'

'Mad,' repeated Black Coll, and he began to run to the rescue as fast as his powerful legs would carry him.

When he came near her, Evleen had almost reached the   20 very edge of the rock. He moved very carefully towards her, meaning to catch her in his arms before she knew he was there. Then he could carry her to safety. But at that moment Evleen turned her head and saw him. She gave a loud scream of hate and fear. A step back brought her within a foot of   25 death.

Black Coll caught her, but one look into her eyes told him he was holding a mad woman. Back, back, she dragged him, and he had nothing to hold on to. The rock was slippery and his shoes would not cling to it. Back, back. There was a   30 scream, a mad swinging to and fro, and then the rock was empty against the sky. No one was there. Black Coll and Evleen Blake lay far below.

2 Two Boxes of Gold

My name is Herbert Blamyre. I live with my wife, Minnie, in
a little house to the south of London. We had only been
married for a month, and had returned from a holiday in
Ireland. I was a junior partner in a bank in Lombard Street,
5 and had four more days of holiday left. Minnie and I were
sitting in the garden, when the maid brought the telegram
which was to start my adventures.

The telegram was from my partner, Mr Schwarzmoor. It
said, 'We want you to start for Italy at once on important
10 business. No delay. Be at office by 6. 30. Start from London
Bridge by 9.15, and catch Dover night boat.'

'Herbert, dear, you won't go, you mustn't go,' said Minnie.
'Please, don't go!'

'I must, my dear,' I said. 'The Bank has no one to send but
15 me. I shall not be gone for long. I must start in ten minutes,
and catch the next train.'

Mr Schwarzmoor met me when at last I reached the bank.

'I hope your wife is well,' he said. 'I am sorry to have to
ask you to miss some of your holiday, but there was nothing
20 I could do about it. We need you to take some gold to Naples.
Here it is,' and he pointed to two large boxes. 'The boxes are
made of iron, but we have covered them with leather, so that
they look like samples. They are fastened with letter-locks,
and contain a quarter of a million pounds in gold. You must
25 take the money to Pagliavicini and Rossi, No. 172 Toledo,
Naples. The king of Naples expects that there will be a war,
and he needs the money to buy guns. The names that open
the locks are "Masinisa", for the one with the white star on
the cover, and "Cotopaxo" for the one with the black star.
30 You must not forget these two words. Open the boxes at
Lyons to make sure all is well. Talk to no one. Do not make
any friends on the way.'

'I shall pretend to be a travelling salesman,' I said.

'Please be careful, Blamyre. You have a dangerous journey ahead of you. Do you have a gun?'

I opened my coat, and showed a special belt with a gun in it.   5

'Good,' said Mr Schwarzmoor. 'I hope you do not need to use it. You will stop in Paris tomorrow. I have some letters for you to give to Lefebre and Desjeans, and you will go on to Marseilles by the night train. You catch the boat on Friday. We will send you a telegram at Marseilles. Are the letters   10
for Paris ready, Mr Hargrave?'

'Yes, sir, nearly ready. Mr. Wilkins is working on them now.'

On the boat from Dover

I reached Dover before midnight, and at once got four porters to carry my chests down the stone steps leading to   15
the Calais boat. The first was taken safely onto the boat, but while the second was being carried down, one of the men slipped. He would have fallen into the water, but he was caught by a large man who, with his wife, was just in front of me.   20

'Steady, my man,' he said. 'Why, what have you got there?'

'Don't know, sir,' replied the porter. 'I only know it's heavy enough to break a man's back.'

'These steps cause a lot of trouble when bringing down heavy goods,' said a voice behind me. 'I see, from your lug-   25
gage, that we may be in the same business.'

I looked round as we stepped on board. The man who had spoken to me was tall and thin. He had a rather large nose, and a long thin face. He wore an overcoat which was too small for him, a flowered waistcoat, tight trousers, a high   30
shirt collar and a stiff neck-cloth.

I replied that I was a travelling salesman, and that I thought we might be going to have a rough journey across to France.

'Yes, a very dirty night,' he said. 'I advise you to find your bed at once. The boat, I see, is very crowded.'

I went straight to my bed, and lay down for an hour. At the end of that time I got up and looked around me. At one of the small tables sat six of the passengers, among them the two I had already met. They were talking and drinking, and I went over to join them. The large man was a Major Baxter, who had been in India for some years. The other was a Mr Levison.

'It's getting very hot down here,' said the Major. 'Why don't we three go up on deck and get some fresh air? My wife is always ill on these crossings. We won't see her again until the boat stops.'

When we got on deck, I saw, to my great surprise, four other cases exactly like mine. I could hardly believe my eyes, but there they were, leather covers, letter-locks and all.

'Those are mine, sir,' said Mr Levison. 'I am travelling for the House of Mackintosh. Those cases contain waterproof overcoat, the best make in the world. We have used these cases for many years. It is sometimes difficult, this accidental resemblance of luggage. It sometimes leads to mistakes. However, I would think your goods are much heavier than mine. What do you carry? Gas pipes, railway chairs, knives, or something else made of iron?'

I did not reply.

'Sir, I think you will do very well,' said Levison. 'Trade secrets should not be discussed in public. Don't you think so, Major?'

'You're right, sir,' replied the Major. 'One cannot be too careful.'

'There's the Calais light,' cried someone at that moment, and soon we were getting ready to leave the boat.

I thought no more about my travelling companions. We parted at Paris. I went my way and they went their way. The Major was going to visit Dromont, near Lyons. From there he would go to Marseilles, then on to Alexandria. Mr Levison was also going to Marseilles, like myself and the Major, but not by my train. He had too much to do in Paris first.

On the train

I had delivered my letters in Paris and was on my way back
to my hotel with Mr Lefebre, a great friend of mine. It was
about six o'clock and we were crossing the road, when a
carriage* passed us. In it was Mr Levison, and his four boxes
were by his side. I waved to him, but he did not seem to   *5*
notice me. In the same street we met the major and his wife,
on their way to the railway station.

'Terrible city, this,' said the Major. 'It smells so of onions.
I'd like to wash it out house by house. Julia, this is my
pleasant travelling companion of last night.' They went on   *10*
their way.

At midnight, I was standing at the station watching my
luggage being put onto the train. A cab* drew up and an
Englishman got out. He asked the driver, in excellent French,
for change for a five-franc piece. It was Levison, but I saw no   *15*
more of him, for the crowd just then pushed me forward.

I found a seat in a carriage with two other people. They
were so wrapped up in their coats that I could not see what
they were like at all.

Once the train had started, I fell asleep and dreamed of my   *20*
dear wife, and our home. Then I began to worry, for I
dreamed I had forgotten the words which would open the
letter-locks. I tried hard to remember, but it was no good.
Then I was in the bank at No. 172 Toledo, Naples, being
ordered to give the words, or be put to death by a row of   *25*
soldiers. I must give the words, or tell where I had hidden the
boxes, for I seemed to have hidden them for some reason. At
that moment an earthquake shook the city, a flood of fire
rolled past beneath the window. I cried out, 'Please God,
show me the words,' and then I woke up.   *30*

'Dromont, Dromont. Ten minutes to Dromont,' called the
guard.

At Dromont I went to the restaurant and asked for a cup of

carriage, four-wheeled vehicle drawn by horses.
cab, horse-drawn taxi.

coffee. Suddenly three or four noisy young Englishmen came hurrying in, with a quiet, elderly travelling salesman. It was Levison again. They led him along, and called for champagne.

'Yes, yes,' the leader said. 'You must have some, old man.
5 We have won three games, you know. You will be able to get your own back before we get to Lyons.'

Levison talked cheerfully about the last game of cards and drank the wine. In a few minutes the young men had drunk their champagne, and gone out to smoke. In another moment
10 Levison caught my eye.

'Why, good gracious,' he said. 'Well, I am glad to see you. Now, my dear sir, you must have some champagne with me.' He called to the waiter, 'Another bottle of champagne, if you please.' Then, turning to me he said, 'I hope to join you
15 before we get to Lyons. I am tired of the noise of those youngsters. Besides, I cannot afford to lose too much money.'

The waiter brought the bottle of champagne. Levison took the bottle at once.
20 'No,' he said, 'I never allow anyone to open wine for me.'

He turned his back on me to remove the wire. He had taken it off, and was filling my glass, when up dashed a man to shake hands with me. He was in such a hurry that he knocked into Mr Levison and the bottle of champagne was
25 broken.

It was the Major, hot, as usual, and very eager to talk to us.

'Oh, I am so sorry. Let me order another bottle. How are you gentlemen? How lucky to meet you again. Julia's with the luggage. We can have a good time here. More champagne
30 here. What's "bottle" in French? Such an annoying thing has happened. Those friends of Julia's have gone off on holiday. They'd forgotten we were coming. Very bad, very bad. Ah, there's the bell. We'll all go in the same carriage.'

Levison looked rather angry. 'I shall not see you for a
35 station or two,' he said. 'I must join those boys, and see if I can win back some of my money. Goodbye, Major Baxter, goodbye Mr Blamyre.'

A surprise stop

I found the Major quite pleasant to talk to. He was full of stories about his days in India, always interrupted by his fussy, good-natured, managing wife.

Soon the train stopped at Charmont, and in came Levison.

'No more heavy losing for me,' he said. 'But if you and the   5
Major and Mrs Baxter would care for a game at a shilling a point, then I'm willing to play.'

We agreed. We cut for partners. I and Mrs Baxter against the Major and Levison. We won nearly every game. Levison played too carefully, and the Major talked and laughed and   10
always forgot which cards had been played.

Still, it helped to pass the time. When we had played for long enough we began to talk. Levison started to tell us about his business.

'I have at last discovered something for which the makers   15
of waterproof clothing have been searching for years,' he said. 'That is, how to let out the heated air of the body, and yet at the same time to keep out the rain. When I get back to London, I shall offer this secret to the Mackintosh firm for ten thousand pounds. If they refuse the offer, I shall at once   20
open a shop in Paris. I shall call the new material Magentosh, and make a lot of money out of it.'

'Very clever,' said the Major.

Mr Levison then turned the conversation to the subject of letter-locks.   25

'I always use the letter-lock myself,' he said. 'My two words are Turlurette and Papagayo. Who would guess them? It would take a very clever thief several hours to work out even one of them. Do you find the letter-lock safe, sir?' he asked, turning to me.   30

I replied that I did, and asked what time our train was due at Lyons.

'We are due at Lyons at 4.30,' said the Major. 'It is now five to four. I don't know why, but I have a feeling that something will happen before we get there. I am always   35 unlucky when travelling. How fast we are travelling! See how the carriage rocks. I am sure we shall have a breakdown before we get to Marseilles.'

I began to feel afraid, but did not show it. Could the Major
5 be planning to do something against me?

'Nonsense, Major, be quiet. That's the way you always spoil a journey,' said his wife.

Then Levison began to talk about his early life. He had been working for a place that made neck-cloths. He talked
10 on and on.

Then the train slowed down, moved on, slowed again and stopped.

The Major put his head out of the window, and shouted to a passing guard.
15 'Where are we?'

'Twenty miles from Lyons. This is Fort Rouge, sir.'

'What is the matter? Anything the matter?'

An English voice answered from the next window.

'A wheel broken, they tell us. We shall have to wait two
20 hours and take all the luggage off onto another van.'

'Good Heavens,' I cried.

Levison put his head out of the window. 'It's true,' he said, drawing it in again. 'Two hours' delay at least, the man says. It's very annoying, but these things happen. We'll have some
25 coffee and another game of cards. We must each look at our own luggage, or, if Mr Blamyre will go and order supper, I will see to it all. But goodness me, what is that shining out there by the station lamps? Hey, you sir, guard, what is happening at the station?'
30 'Those are soldiers, sir,' replied the guard. 'They happened to be at the station on their way to Chalons. The station-master has sent them to watch the luggage-van, and to see to the changing over of the luggage. No passenger is to go near it, because there are special government stores in the train.'
35 Levison spat on the ground, and said something under his breath. I supposed he was angry with the French railways.

'I say, sir,' said the Major, 'have you ever seen such clumsy

carts?' and he pointed out of the window. I looked and saw
two country carts, each with four strong horses, that were
standing under a hedge close to the station.

Levison and I tried to get near our luggage, but the soldiers
refused to let us get too close. I watched my chests lifted into   *5*
the new luggage van. I saw no sign of government stores, and
I told the Major so.

'Oh, they're clever,' he replied, 'very clever. It may be the
empress's jewels, only a tiny packet, perhaps, but still not
difficult to steal on a night such as this.'   *10*

Just then there was a loud, high whistle, as if a signal had
been given. The horses in the two carts started off at a gallop
and were soon out of sight.

Marseilles at last

Three hours later we reached Lyons and changed trains for
Marseilles.   *15*

'I shall have a sleep, gentlemen,' said the Major. 'I suppose
the next thing will be the boat breaking down.'

'Major, do please be quiet,' said his wife.

I fell asleep at last, but again my dreams were bad. I
imagined I was in a city where there were narrow, dark   *20*
streets. I was being watched from behind curtained windows.
Four men on horses came riding down the street. They were
waving swords, and were coming towards me. I dreamed I
had only one hope of safety, and that was to repeat the
words of my letter-locks. Already the horses were on top of   *25*
me. I cried out with great difficulty, 'Cotopaxo, Cotopaxo.'
A rough shake woke me. It was the Major.

'You're talking in your sleep,' he said. 'Why do you talk in
your sleep? It's a dangerous habit.'

'What was I talking about?' I asked.   *30*

'Some foreign nonsense,' replied the Major.

'Greek, I think,' said Levison, 'but I can't be sure.'

We reached Marseilles. I was so happy to see the white
houses and the almond trees. I should feel safer when I was

on the ship, and my treasure with me. I had noticed that on
that long journey from Lyons I had been watched. I had
never fallen asleep without waking to find either the Major,
or his wife, or Levison looking at me.

5   We agreed to keep together, and stood by our luggage
trying to decide which hotel to stay at.

'Hotel Imperial is the best,' said the Major. But the Hotel
Imperial was full.

'Oh, no,' said the Major. 'The boat will be the next thing
10   to fail.'

And it was. There had been an accident with the boiler,
and it would not leave until half an hour after midnight.

'Where shall we go?' I asked. 'Our journey seems very
unlucky so far. Let's have dinner together. I must send a
15   message first, but then I'm free until half past eleven.'

'I will take you to a small, but very good hotel down by
the harbour,' said Levison. 'The Foreigners' Hotel.'

'It's not a very good place,' said the Major, who knew it
well.

20   'Sir,' said Mr Levison, 'it is under new management, or I
would not have suggested it to you.'

'I'm sorry,' said the Major, 'I did not know that.'

We entered the hotel, and found it was rather bare and not
too clean.

25   'I shall go and wash, and then take a walk while you go
and send your messages,' said the Major. 'You go and see to
the rooms, Julia.'

'I am going to try and get to the shops before they shut,'
said Levison.

30   There were only two double-bedded rooms left.

'That will do,' said Levison, quickly. 'My friend is going on
the boat tonight. He will not be sleeping here. His luggage can
be put in my room, and he can take the key, in case he comes
in first.'

35   'Then now we are all right,' said the Major. 'So far, so
good.'

When I got to the telegraph office, I found a telegram

waiting for me from London. To my surprise and horror it
contained only these words:

'You are in great danger. Do not wait a moment on shore.
There is a plot against you. Go to the police and ask for a
guard.'   5

It must be the Major. I was in his hands. That friendly
manner of his was all a trick. Even now he might be carrying
off the chests. I sent a message back.

'Safe at Marseilles. All right up to this.'

I ran back to the hotel, which was in a dirty street by the   10
harbour. As I turned the corner into the street, a man came
out of a doorway and took my arm. It was one of the men
from the hotel. He said hurriedly in French, 'Quick, quick,
sir. Major Baxter wants to see you at once in the dining-
room. There is no time to lose.'   15

To catch a thief

I ran to the hotel, and hurried into the dining-room. There
was the Major, walking up and down in great excitement. His
wife was looking out of the window. The Major ran up and
took my hand.

'I am a police officer, and my name is Arnott,' he said.   20
'That man Levison is a well-known thief. He is, at this
moment, opening one of your chests. You must help me to
catch him. I knew what he was going to do, but I wanted to
catch him in the act. Have you got a gun, Mr Blamyre, in case
he puts up a fight? I have a strong stick.'   25

'I have left my gun in the bedroom,' I said.

'That's bad. Never mind, he may not think of it. You must
rush at the door at the same moment as I do. These foreign
locks are never any good. It's No. 15. Quietly now.'

We came to the door. We listened a moment. We could   30
hear the sound of money clinking in a bag. Then Levison
laughed over the word he had heard me say in my sleep.
'Cotopaxo, ha, ha.'

The Major gave the word and we both rushed at the door.

It shook, broke and opened. Levison, with a revolver in his
hand, stood over the open box, ankle deep in gold. He had
already filled a huge belt that was round his waist, and a bag
that hung at his side. Another bag, half full, lay at his feet.
He did not say one word. There were ropes at the window,   5
as if he had been lowering, or preparing to lower, bags into
the side street. He gave a whistle, and some vehicle could be
heard driving away fast.

'Give yourself up. I know you,' cried the Major. 'Give up,
I've got you now.'   10

Levison's only reply was to fire the gun. Luckily for us,
nothing happened. I had forgotten to load it.

Levison threw it at the Major in anger, quickly opened the
window and jumped out.

I went out after him, shouting for help. Arnott stayed to   15
guard the money.

A moment more and a wild crowd of soldiers, sailors and
other men were following Levison. In the half-dark, (the
lamps were just being lit), we raced after him. Hundreds of
blows were aimed at him, hundreds of hands stretched out to   20
catch him. He got away from one, knocked another down
and jumped over a third. We had almost caught him, when
suddenly his foot caught on something and he fell head-first
into the harbour. There was a shout as he splashed and disappeared into the dark water. I ran down the nearest steps   25
and waited while the police took a boat and dragged with
hooks for the body.

'They are clever, these old thieves. I remember this man
here at Toulon. I knew his face in a moment. He has dived
under the ships and got into some boat and hidden himself.   30
'You'll never see him again,' said an old grey-haired police-
man who had taken me into the boat.

'Yes we shall, for here he is,' cried a second, bending down
and lifting a body out of the water by the hair.

'Oh, he was a clever one,' said a man from a boat behind   35
us. It was Arnott. 'Just came to see how you were getting on,
sir. Don't worry about the money. Julia's watching it. I often

said that man would be caught some day. He nearly had you,
Mr Blamyre. He'd have cut your throat while you were
asleep, rather than miss the money. But I was on his track.
He didn't know me. Well, his name is off the books now.
5 That's one good thing. Come, my friends, bring that body to
land. We must strip him of the money he has upon him. It at
least did one good thing while he had it. It sent him to the
bottom of the harbour.'

Arnott told me everything when we returned to the hotel.
10 On the night I had started my journey, he had received orders
from the London head office to follow me, and watch
Levison. He had not had time to tell my partners. The driver
of our train had been paid to make the engine break down at
Fort Rouge, where Levison's men were waiting with the
15 carts. They planned to carry off the luggage in the darkness.
This plan failed, because Arnott had sent a message from
Paris for soldiers to be sent to the station. The champagne he
had spilt had been drugged. Levison, defeated the first time,
had tried other ways. My unlucky talk in my sleep had given
20 him the power of opening one of the chests. The breakdown
of the boat, which was quite accidental (as far as we could
tell), gave him a last chance.

That night, thanks to Arnott, I left Marseilles with not one
single piece of money lost. The rest of my journey was good.
25 Our bank has done well ever since, and so have Minnie and I.

3 George and Geoffrey

Cumner is a very pretty village in England. It has one short street of small houses, a police station, a post-office and an old inn. Facing you, as you enter the street, is the lovely old church. There is a large grassy space, called The Common, which has houses on three sides of it. There is a butcher's shop, the big house belonging to Mr Malcolmson, and a small house where Simon Eade, who works for Mr Malcolmson, lives with his wife and son. And there is Mr Gibbs's house, behind a high brick wall.

George Eade was a good-looking young man of twenty-six. He also worked for Mr Malcolmson, and was honest and hard-working. However, he did not make friends easily, and had a very bad temper at times.

Mrs Eade loved her son very much. She was, therefore, rather jealous when she found out that George was in love with, and meant to marry, Susan Archer. She did not like the girl very much.

Susan was the daughter of a farmer. Her parents managed a large farm belonging to Sir Oswald Dunstan, and they thought that their daughter was too good for the son of one of Mr Malcolmson's workers. The young couple had met in the fields. The girl had been unwell for some time, and her doctor had said it would do her good to have a holiday in the open air. Now there were not many places that her parents thought fit to send her. But they knew and liked the Eades, so she was sent to Mr Malcolmson's fields. She got better at once, but she also fell in love.

George had never cared for a woman before, and he fell deeply in love with Susan. They promised to marry as soon as they could.

Geoffrey

But there was at this time a man called Geoffrey Gibbs, who was interested in Susan, and wanted to make her his wife. He had been left his house by a relation who had died some years ago, and lived like a lord. The Archers thought
5 he would be much better for Susan, and told her so, many times. However, she did not like him, and had been heard to say that if he were ten times as rich, she would die rather than be married to the ugly monster.

And he was ugly, not only in looks, but in his manner too.
10 His legs were short, and his body and hands were long. He had a very large head, which gave him a top-heavy appearance. He had large eye-brows and nasty, small eyes. His nose was shaped like a beak, and he had a huge mouth.

George and Geoffrey disliked each other very much. Gibbs
15 hated George because Susan loved him.

As soon as Mr Malcolmson heard that George and Susan were soon to be married, he raised the young man's wages. He also said he would repair a small house for the young couple, which belonged to him, but was not far from Simon
20 Eade's house.

When Gibbs heard of the coming wedding, he was very angry and jealous. He went at once to see Mr Archer, promising to give Susan a lot of money if she would forget George and marry him instead. Mr Archer would have liked to have
25 been able to make Susan change her mind, but he could not.

Susan was very upset. She told George what had happened, and he was angry.

'Does your father think money is more important than true love?' he said. 'If I thought you would be happier with
30 Gibbs than me, I would give you up. But you would be very unhappy. He's mean and cruel. He couldn't make any woman happy. I'll work hard for you, Susan, you'll see. We too may have money like his some day.'

'I don't want money, George,' said Susan, 'I'm happy with
35 you the way you are.'

They agreed that, to keep her out of Gibbs's way until the wedding, she should go and stay with her aunt at Orminston. She went away, and so did George. He went to buy some furniture at a sale on the other side of the country. It was nice for him to be away too, for his mother seemed to be   5
growing more against his marriage every day.

Where is Susan?

When George returned from his holiday he expected to find a letter from Susan waiting for him. He wanted to know when she would be coming back. But there was no letter. Instead, there was a note. It said: 10

George Eade, you are being cheated. Look to G.G.
                                    A WELL-WISHER.

George was worried. He did not feel any better when he found that Gibbs had also left Cumner the day after himself, and was still away.   15

Next morning, his mother handed him a letter. It was from Farmer Archer, and contained a letter from his sister. In her letter, she told him that her niece, Susan, had left her house secretly two days before, to be married to Mr Gibbs. It seemed that the girl had gone to spend the day with a cousin,   20
as she had done before. When she did not return that night, her aunt thought that she must have decided to sleep at her cousin's place. Next morning, she had received news of the marriage.

When he read this, George could not believe it. There must   25
be some mistake. It could not be true. But half an hour later, James Wilkins, Mr Gibbs's man-servant, brought another letter. It was from Susan, and signed with her new name.

It said: *I know that you will never forgive me for what I have done. I have behaved very badly to you, and I can't ask*   30
you to forgive me. But I do ask you to do nothing about trying to find me, or taking revenge. It cannot bring back the past. Forget all about me. That's the best thing for both of

us. It would have been better if we had never met.

He looked at the letter, then, without a word, held it out
to his father. He left the room. They heard him go up the
stairs and lock himself in his bedroom, and they heard no
5 more.

After a while his mother went to him. Although she felt
glad that he had not after all married Susan, she knew how he
must be feeling.

'Have patience, son,' she said. 'She wasn't good enough for
10 you, you know. I always said so.'

'Mother, I don't want to hear another word about her
from now on. What she's done isn't so bad, after all. I'm all
right. You won't see any difference in me, at least, not if
you'll stop talking about her and using her name, ever again.
15 She's turned my heart to stone, that's all.'

He put his hand on his chest and gave a great sigh. 'This
morning I had a heart of flesh here,' he said, 'now it's cold,
heavy stone. But it doesn't matter.'

'Oh, don't speak like that,' his mother cried. She burst into
20 tears and threw her arms around him. He gently pushed her
away, kissed her on the cheek, and led her to the door. 'I
must go to work now,' he said, and went down the stairs.

From that day, no one heard him speak of Susan Gibbs.
He never spoke of them or of her, to his relations or to hers.
25 Susan appeared to be, for him, as if she had never been.

Susan's return

From that awful day, he was a changed man. He worked as
hard and carefully as ever, but no man ever saw him smile, or
heard him laugh. He stayed away from everyone, except his
parents. He was now a sad and lonely man.

30 Mr Gibbs's house on The Common was rented out to
strangers, and for nearly three years nothing was seen of him
or his wife. Then news came one day that they were returning to Cumner, and there was soon an air of excitement in
the small village. They came back and certain things that had

been heard about them over the years were found to be true.
Word had got around, as words sometimes do, that Gibbs
treated his wife very badly. Her father and brothers, who had
been to visit them more than once, were strangely silent
about those visits. It was well known now, that Farmer   5
Archer was sorry that his daughter had married Gibbs, even
though he had been in favour of the marriage before. No one
was surprised when they saw her. She was thin and pale. She
hardly ever smiled, except when she played with her son. He
was a lovely, fair-haired child, and looked just like her. But   10
his father was often unkind to him.
    It was some time before George met Susan again. He never
went out, except to work, and she never left her house
except to drive with her husband, or to walk to her father's
farm. Although George never spoke of her, or watched for   15
her, he could not help hearing things that were said about the
Gibbses. The men at work talked of the husband's cruelty.
The baker's boy had many tales of the bad words he had
heard and the blows he had been given when Gibbs was too
drunk to know what he was doing.   20
    One Sunday, the Eades were sitting at the table eating
their one o'clock lunch, when they heard the sound of a
carriage being driven past. It was going very fast. Mrs Eade
went to the window.
    'I thought so,' she cried. 'It's Gibbs driving to Tenelms,   25
and he's drunk again. See how he's hitting the horse. And
he's got the little boy with him too. He won't be happy until
he's broken that child's neck, or the mother's.'
    George had also come to the window, and stood looking
after the carriage.   30
    'I wish he might break his own neck,' George said, between
his teeth.
    'Oh, George, don't say such a thing,' cried Mrs Eade, with
a pale shocked face.
    'If you went to church, my boy, instead of keeping away,'   35
said his father, 'you might have better feelings in your heart.'
    'Church,' cried George. 'I was going there once, and it

wasn't allowed. I'll not go there again. Do you think because
I'm quiet, that I've forgotten? Forgotten,' he banged his hand
down hard on the table. 'I'll tell you when I shall forget. I
shall be lying white and stiff in my coffin. Leave me alone,
5 and it would be best for us all if you never spoke that man's
name again.' He went out of the room, and out of the house.

The accident

It was well known, in the village, that Mrs Gibbs was
always afraid for the safety of her son. Her husband was
always driving the little boy out in the carriage, far too fast.
10 There had been many ugly scenes between the parents
because of this. The more Susan cried and begged him to
stop, the worse he became. One day, to frighten her still
more, he put the little boy into the carriage alone. He stood
him on the seat with a whip in his hands, and stood at the
15 door, holding the reins loosely in his hand. He was laughing
at his wife, who kept begging him to get in, or let her do so.
Suddenly there was a bang from a gun in a nearby field. The
horse was frightened, and started off wildly, pulling the reins
out of the father's hands as it did so. The whip fell from the
20 child's hands onto the back of the horse, making it even more
excited. And the boy was thrown screaming to the bottom of
the carriage, where he lay still, too frightened to move.

George was close by when all this happened. He threw
himself on the flying horse, and held onto its reins with all
25 his strength. He was dragged along, until at last the animal
caught its legs in the reins and fell. George was thrown to
the ground, but was unhurt except for a few cuts and bruises.
The child at the bottom of the carriage, though frightened
and screaming, was completely unhurt. In less than five
30 minutes half the village had collected to find out what had
happened. Susan, holding her child in her arms, came crying
up to George.

'Bless you, bless you,' she cried. 'You saved my little boy's
life. He might have been killed but for you. How can I ever
35 . . .'

But a rough hand pushed her aside. 'What are you doing now?' Gibbs was heard to cry. 'Leave that man alone, or I'll . . . Are you making a fool of yourself in this way, because he's lamed the horse so that it will have to be shot?'

5   The poor girl sat down on the bank and cried, while a shout of, 'Shame, shame,' rose among the people watching.

George Eade had turned coldly from Susan when she rushed up to him. Now, in front of Gibbs he said, 'It'll be a good deed done, whoever shoots that horse of yours. And it 10 would be better still to shoot *you* as a man would a mad dog.'

All heard these words. All shook with fear as he spoke them. The anger of the last three years showed in that one look of terrible hatred.

Oh, George, what have you done?

15   Two days later, Mr Murray, the priest, came to visit Mrs Eade. He wanted to tell her how pleased he was that George had not been hurt in the accident. He found her very worried. George's words had frightened her so badly that she could not sleep. The priest had tried to talk to George, to get him 20 to come to church, and forget the hate he felt in his heart, but it was no use. George answered rudely that, as long as he did his work properly, and hurt no one, he had a right to decide for himself things which were his own business. And one of his decisions was never to go inside a church again.

25   'It's very sad,' said Mr Murray to Mrs Eade, 'and hard for you to bear. But have faith. There is hidden good in it that we can't see now.'

'It would be strange if I wasn't glad that he had been unhurt,' said Mrs Eade, 'but it's terrible to have him looking 30 so unforgiving and full of hate as he does now.'

She stopped talking as there was a knock on the door. The son of Mr Beach, the butcher, looked in at the door. He looked fearfully from one to the other.

'I don't want anything this morning, thank you, Jim,' said

Mrs Eade. Then, noticing the strange look on the young man's face, she added, 'Isn't Mr Beach very well this morning? You look very strange.'

'I don't feel too well,' the boy replied. 'I've just been to look at *him,* and it made me feel sick.'   5

'Him? Who?'

'Why, haven't you heard? Gibbs has been found dead in Southanger Woods. Murdered last night, they say.'

'Gibbs murdered?'

There was a pause of breathless horror.   10

'They carried his body to the inn, and I saw it.'

Mrs Eade turned deathly pale. Soon the house was full of people, though why they had come to the Eades's house, wasn't quite clear. Everyone was talking about the murder. How had it been done, and why? Into the middle of all the   15 noise and questions walked George Eade.

There was a sudden silence. He must have noticed it as he came in through the door.

There was no need to ask if he knew what had happened. His face, pale as death, showed that he had heard the terrible   20 news. But his first words, spoken very softly, were to be remembered for a very long time.

'I WISH I'D BEEN FOUND DEAD IN THAT WOOD IN-STEAD OF GIBBS.'

I did not do it

There were many reasons why George was thought to have   25 been the one who had killed Gibbs. His father did not believe that George was guilty, and was sure that it would soon be proved that his son could not have done such a terrible thing. When the police arrived to take George away for questioning, he went without a fuss, but said that he had nothing to fear   30 as he had done nothing wrong.

The body of the dead man had been found at about ten a.m., by a farmer. It lay by the side of a path in the woods. There were signs that there had been a fight. There was blood,

too, which must have come from the wound on the back of
the dead man's head. He must have been struck from behind
by something very heavy. When he was found, he had been
dead for about eleven or twelve hours. His pockets were
5   empty, and a watch, purse and ring were missing.

Gibbs's two servants said that their master left the house
on the night of the murder, at twenty minutes past eight. He
had not been drinking. He had said that he would go to the
inn first, and then to his wife's home. They had not worried
10 when he did not come home that night, because he was often
away until morning, and he had a key with him.

Simon Eade, his wife and servant all said that George returned home on the night of the murder, at nine o'clock. He
had been out since tea-time, and there was nothing unusual
15 about his looks or speech when he came in. He stayed with
his family until ten, when they all went to bed. The servant
saw him come downstairs in the morning, quite early.

There was a cut on his left hand, which he said had been
caused when his knife slipped as he was cutting some bread.
20 There was blood on his coat, which he said he had got on it
when he cut his hand. The only thing belonging to the dead
man that was found on him was a small pencil, marked with
"G.G.", and three small cuts. Job Brettle, the blacksmith, said
that Gibbs had given him the pencil and asked him to make
25 the cuts, on the afternoon of the murder. He (Brettle) had
noticed the letters at the same time, and was sure that this
was the pencil he had cut. George said he had picked it up on
The Common, and had no idea to whom it belonged.

It was then learned that there had been a very bad quarrel
30 between Mr and Mrs Gibbs on the morning of the murder.
After it, she had been heard to say that she could not bear it
any more, and would go for help to someone who would not
refuse it. She had sent a letter to George Eade, by the son of
a villager, and had gone out herself at night, a few minutes
35 after her husband. She had returned fifteen minutes later,
and had gone up to her bedroom, and had not left the room
until the next morning.

When the judge questioned her about where she had been that night, she would not answer.

George admitted that he had gone to the Southanger Woods at about twenty minutes to eight on the night of the murder, but he refused to give any reason for going there. He had only been about fifteen minutes, he said. He also said that, as he was coming back along the path, he saw Gibbs and his dog coming towards him, but far away. The moon was very bright and he recognized him at once. He didn't want to meet him, so went home another way, reaching the house at about nine o'clock without meeting anyone on the way.

There were now three points in George's favour:

1. Three people had seen him return home at nine o'clock, and sit down to supper showing no signs of hurry or fear.
2. The shortness of the time in which he could have done the terrible deed, and hidden the stolen property.
3. The good manner in which he had lived up until now.

The points against him were:

1. The cut on his hand, and marks of blood on his coat.
2. Gibbs's pencil, found upon him.
3. The fact that he would not say what he had been doing during the thirty minutes that passed between Gibbs leaving the inn, and his (George's) return home.
4. The terrible hate he was known to have felt for the dead man, and certain words he had been heard to speak, showing he wished him dead.

George stood calmly while all the questions were being asked. He never once let it be seen how he was feeling. It was arranged that he should be properly tried by judge and jury during the next month.

His trial will be remembered for a long time in Cumner. There was a lot of excitement about it, not only in the village, but all over the county. Mr Malcolmson, who never could believe that George was guilty, spent a lot of money in getting good lawyers for him.

He stood calmly in court, looking very much thinner and older. When the court's decision, not guilty, was heard, a great sigh went round the court-room. Silently, George Eade
5 left the court and went home with his father.

People expected that he would leave Cumner after this, and go to live and work somewhere else. But he did not. On the first Sunday after the trial, he went to church. Everyone was very surprised. He had become very quiet in his manner,
10 working hard all day, and reading to himself at night. He never spoke of the past, but he never forgot it.

He and Susan never met. For a long time she lay dangerously ill at her father's house.

Luke Williams

About twelve months after all these things happened, Mr
15 Murray, the priest, was sitting in his library alone. There was a knock on the door, and a servant came in. He told Mr Murray that a man calling himself Luke Williams wanted to speak with him. It was past ten o'clock, and the clergyman was ready to go to bed.
20 'Tell him to come tomorrow morning,' he said. 'It's too late to talk now.'

'I did tell him so, sir, but he said that what he has to say can't wait.'

'Is he a beggar?'
25 'He didn't ask for anything sir, but he looks very poor.'

'Show him in.'

The man entered. He looked terrible. He was pale, hollow-eyed, and so thin. He had a nasty cough which made him pant and gasp for breath. He looked very ill. He turned to Mr
30 Murray and looked at him sadly.

'Well?'

The stranger looked quickly at the servant.

'Leave the room, Robert,' said Mr Murray.

Robert did so, but stayed very close outside.

'This is a strange hour to come to talk to me. Have you
something important to say?'

'It is a strange hour, sir, for coming, but my reason for
coming is stranger.'

The man turned to the window and looked at the full 5
October moon which lit up the sky.

'Well?' said Mr Murray once more.

But the man's eyes were fixed on the sky.

'Yes,' he said, shaking, 'it shone like that the night of the
murder. It shone on Gibbs's face, as he lay there. It shone 10
on his open eyes. I couldn't get them to shut. I've never seen
moonlight like that since, till tonight. And I'm here to give
myself up to you. I always felt I should, and it's better done
and over.'

'You murdered Gibbs? You?' 15

'I did. I've been there tonight, to look at the place. I felt I
must see it again. And I saw his eyes, as plain as I see you,
open, with the moon shining on them. A horrible sight.'

'You look very wild and ill. Perhaps . . . '

'You don't believe me. I wish I didn't believe myself. See 20
here.'

With shaking fingers he took from his pocket the watch,
purse and ring that had belonged to Gibbs. He laid them on
the table, and Mr Murray knew them.

'I used the money,' said the man, faintly. 'There wasn't 25
much, and I needed it badly.'

Then he sat down on a chair and began to groan. Mr
Murray gave him something to drink, and he began to tell his
story.

He and Gibbs had once worked together in a money 30
lending business. The business had been bad, and Williams
had lost all his money. Gibbs had offered to help him, if he
would agree to help in a plan to steal Susan away from
George Eade. When she and George had parted for the two
weeks before their wedding, Gibbs and Williams had followed 35
her to Ormiston. They had watched her closely. They found
out that she was going to spend a day with her cousin, and

sent a woman after her with a message. The message was
supposed to have come from George. It told her to come
quickly to him, as he had been in an accident and was badly
hurt. He might only have a few hours to live. The poor girl
5 was so upset, that she followed the woman to a house outside
town. When she entered the house, she found Gibbs and
Williams waiting for her. They told her it was no use her
screaming for help, because she would not be heard. She
must promise to marry Gibbs, or she would never be set free.
10 Gibbs added that, if she had married George, he would have
had him killed on the way back from the church.

At first Susan refused to agree. But she was watched all
day and night, and Gibbs stood over her with a loaded gun,
frightening her so much that she at last gave in. She wrote the
15 letters to her aunt, and to George, but was only allowed to
put down on paper what Gibbs told her to say. She was
married three weeks later. Even then, Williams said, she
would have refused, but for her fears for George's safety. His
life seemed more important to her than her own. Then
20 Williams asked for his reward.

However, his wicked friend was not willing to pay all the
money he had promised. He paid some of it, but refused the
rest. Williams was in great trouble, and went down to
Cumner, hoping to see Gibbs. He did see him one night, as
25 Gibbs was driving home drunk from Tenelms. Gibbs, however, was not too drunk to recognize Williams, and tried to
drive his horse over him. Williams, very angry at such treat-
ment, wrote him a letter. In it he said that Gibbs must bring,
on a certain night to a certain place in Southhanger Woods,
30 every bit of the money he had promised to pay. If he failed,
then Williams would go to the police the next morning, and
tell them all about the way in which Susan had become Mrs
Gibbs.

Gibbs was frightened by this letter, and went to meet
35 Williams, but without taking the money. It soon became clear
that Gibbs was not going to pay him anything, so Williams,
getting very angry, said he would take whatever valuables

Gibbs had on his person. A fight began, during which Gibbs tried to hurt Williams with a knife. At last, Williams managed to throw Gibbs to the ground. He used such strength that Gibbs's head hit a tree with such a blow that it killed him. Very frightened by what he had done, Williams had dragged *5* the body to the side of the path, taken the things out of the pockets and run off. The church clock struck ten as he came out of the woods. He had walked all that night, rested the next day, and managed to reach London undiscovered. But he was almost immediately arrested by the police, for debts *10* that he could not pay. He had been in prison until a few days ago, when he was set free. He was now very ill, and probably dying.

A happy ending

This, then, was the story, told in whispers to the priest by that poor man. It was a story impossible to disbelieve, and it *15* cleared the name of one who had been for too long thought guilty. Before twelve o'clock the next day, the whole village knew about Williams's story.

Susan was better now, and able to say that what Williams had told the priest about her marriage to Gibbs was all true. *20* She also told about the letter she had sent to George on the day of the murder. It had been to ask him to go and see her father, and get him to see lawyers for her. She wanted a separation from her husband, but was watched too closely to be able to do anything for herself. And as her letters were *25* often opened by her husband, she asked George to meet her in Southanger Woods that night to tell her the results. But Susan, learning that Gibbs was going through the woods that night, had rushed out to warn George, and prevent the two from meeting, which they very nearly did. *30*

So once more Susan and George met. There is a small house on Cumner Common, not far from Simon Eade's. There you may see Susan, happy now with her brown-eyed baby in her arms. And you may also see George Eade, coming in to dinner or tea, tall and handsome and with a smile on his face. So, all's well that ends well.

4 A Ghost Story

I cannot explain the story I am about to tell. Nothing quite
like it has ever happened to me before, and I hope will never
happen again.

A few years ago, it does not matter how many, a murder
was done in England which caused great excitement. When   *5*
the murder was first discovered, no one suspected the man
who was afterwards brought to trial. Nothing was said about
him in the newspapers at that time, and no description of
him was ever given. It is very important that this fact be
remembered.   *10*

One morning at breakfast, I opened my newspaper and
found the story of that first discovery. I thought it was very
interesting, and read it very carefully. I read it twice, if not
three times. The discovery had been made in a bedroom, and
when I laid down the paper something strange happened to   *15*
me. It was as if I could see that bedroom clearly before my
eyes. It seemed to pass through my room like a picture
painted on a running river. It was so real that I clearly
noticed, thankfully, the absence of the dead body from the
bed.   *20*

I got up and went to the window to get some fresh air, for
I felt very strange. As I looked down into the street, my
rooms being on the second floor, I noticed two men on the
opposite side of the road, going from West to East. They
were one behind the other. The first man often looked back   *25*
over his shoulder. The second man followed him at a distance
of about thirty feet. He had his right hand raised in a
threatening way. First, the strangeness of his threatening
action in such a public place, attracted my attention. Then,
the fact that no one else seemed to notice it. Both men made   *30*
their way among the other people on the street. Nobody that
I could see made way for them, touched them or even looked

at them. As they passed my windows, they both looked up at me. I saw their faces very clearly, and I knew that I would know them again, anywhere. The first man had a bad-tempered look on his face and the second man's face was the colour of wax. 5

An unexpected visitor

As the days passed, more facts about the murder became known. I tried not to show too great an interest in them, but I did know that the suspected murderer had been sent to prison to wait for his trial. I also knew that his trial had been delayed, because time was needed to prepare his defence. 10

My sitting-room, bedroom, and dressing-room are all on one floor. There is no way into my dressing-room except through my bedroom. There is a door in it, which used to lead out onto the staircase, but some years ago a bath was put in my dressing-room, and the door had to be closed up 15 because it got in the way. It had been nailed up and papered over.

I was standing in my bedroom one night, giving some orders to my servant before he went to bed. My face was to-wards the only door into my dressing-room, and it was 20 closed. My servant's back was towards that door. While I was speaking to him I saw it open, and a man looked in. He beckoned* to me, and I noticed that he looked exactly like the man I had seen in the street whose face was the colour of wax. 25

The man, having beckoned, drew back and closed the door. At once I picked up a candle and crossed the bedroom. I opened the dressing-room door and looked in. There was nobody there.

I knew that my servant must be surprised by my behaviour. 30 I turned round to him and said, 'Derrick, could you believe that I just thought I saw a . . .' I put my hand on his arm, and

*beckon, to make a sign with the hand which invites someone to come closer.

he jumped back. 'O yes, sir. A dead man beckoning.'

Now, I do not believe that John Derrick, my trusted servant for more than twenty years, had had any feelings of having seen any such figure, until I touched him. The change
5 in him was so surprising when I touched him, that I am sure he got this feeling in some unknown way from me.

I told him to go and get some brandy, and I gave him a glass. I was glad to drink some myself. I did not tell him anything of what had happened before. On thinking about it, I
10 was certain that I had never seen that face before, except that one time in the street.

I was not very comfortable that night, though for some unexplained reason I was sure that the figure would not come back. At daylight I fell into a heavy sleep. I was wakened by
15 John Derrick coming to my bedside with a paper in his hand.

Called to court

The paper John Derrick brought me had just been delivered to the door. It was an order for me to serve on a jury*
at the next meeting of the Criminal Court of the Old Bailey.
20 I had never been called for jury duty before.

On the morning I had to attend the court, it was very foggy. I *think* that until I was taken by officers into the court room, I did not know that the murderer was to be tried that day.

25 I sat down with the rest of the people who had been called for jury duty and waited. Soon after, the two judges came in and the court was quiet. An order was given to bring in the prisoner. He appeared, and I knew him at once. It was the first of the two men I had seen going down the street.

30 If my name had been called then, I don't think I could have answered. But I was eighth on the list, and by that time I was able to say 'Here.' I stood up and stepped into the jury

*jury, group of people who decide whether someone is innocent or
    guilty at a trial.

box. Now, until that time, the prisoner had been watching
things calmly, but as soon as I stood up, he seemed to get
very worried. He signalled to his lawyer and there was a pause
while they whispered together. At last the lawyer shook his
head. It was clear that the prisoner did not want me on the   5
jury. I found out later that his first words to the lawyer were,
'You must change that man.' But he would give no reason for
it, and said that he had not even known my name until he
had heard it called and I stood up. So I stayed where I was in
the jury box.   10

I was chosen leader of the jury. On the second morning of
the trial, after evidence had been taken for about two hours,
I sat back and looked at my fellow jurymen. I counted them,
but found it very difficult. I counted them several times, yet
every time the number was wrong. I made them one too   15
many.

I asked the man sitting next to me to count too. He looked
surprised, but turned his head and counted. 'Why,' he said,
suddenly, 'we are thirteen . . . . But no, it's not possible. No.
We are twelve.' It was very strange.   20

The jury had to keep together until the end of the trial
and a room had been prepared for us at the London Tavern.
We all slept in one large room on separate beds, and we were
always watched by an officer, who had promised to look
after us carefully. His name was Mr Harker. When we went to   25
sleep at night, Mr Harker's bed was drawn across the door.
On the night of the second day, I did not feel like lying
down. I saw Mr Harker sitting on his bed and went over to
talk to him. I offered him some tobacco from my box. As he
reached to get it, his hand touched mine. He gave a sudden   30
shiver, and said, 'Who is this?'

I followed the direction of his eyes, and looking along the
room, I saw again the figure I expected. It was the second of
the two men who had walked down the street. I got up,
walked forward a few steps, then turned back to Mr Harker.   35
He was laughing now. 'I thought for a moment we had a
thirteenth juryman, without a bed. But I see now it was only

the moonlight,' he said.

I did not say anything to Mr Harker about the man, but invited him to take a walk with me to the end of the room. I watched what the stranger did. He stood for a few minutes
5 by the bed of each juryman, close to the pillow. He always went to the right side of the bed and stood just looking down thoughtfully. He took no notice of me, or of my bed, which was nearest to Mr Harker's. He seemed to go out where the moonlight came in, through a high window, as if by an
10 invisible stairway.

Next morning at breakfast, it seemed that everyone present had dreamed of the murdered man last night, except myself and Mr Harker.

I was now sure that the second man who had gone down
15 the street was the murdered man. It was as clear to me as if he had told me so himself.

On the fifth day of the trial, when the case against the prisoner was coming to an end, a small picture of the murdered man was put up as evidence. It had been missing from
20 the room at the time when the body had been found. But it was found later in a place where the murderer had been seen digging. It was shown to the judges first, and then handed down to the jury. As an officer in a black gown was coming across to me, the figure of the second man who had gone
25 down the street suddenly came out from the crowd. It caught the picture from the officer and gave it to me with its own hands. At the same time it said in a low, hollow voice, 'I was younger then, and my face was not then drained of blood.' It then came between me and the next juryman to whom I
30 would have given the picture, and between him and the juryman to whom he would have given it. And so it passed the picture on through the whole of our jury and back to me. Not one of them, however, noticed anything wrong.

Of course, as we were shut up together, the jurymen and I
35 talked a great deal about the case. On the fifth day, the case against the prisoner was closed. We now knew the facts about him, and our talk was very serious. Among the jurymen there

was one whom I thought very stupid. He had two followers, and the three of them seemed to think that the prisoner might not have done the murder at all. At about midnight, when the three of them were talking very loudly, I again saw the murdered man. He stood behind them, beckoning to me.   *5* When I went towards them and began to talk, he went away. This was the beginning of a separate set of appearances, which happened in that room in which we were kept. Whenever a group of my fellow jurymen got together talking, he would appear amongst them. Whenever they seemed to be   *10* talking against him, he would beckon to me.

It must be remembered that until the fifth day of the trial, when the picture of the murdered man was shown to the jury, I had never seen the ghost in court. As the case for the defence began, it was in the court-room every day. However,   *15* it did not take any notice of me now but always stood by the person who was talking at the time. For example, the throat of the murdered man had been cut straight across. In the opening speech for the defence, it was suggested that the dead man might have cut his own throat. At that very   *20* moment, the figure, with its throat in the terrible condition just described, stood at the speaker's elbow. It made movements across its wind-pipe, now with the right hand, now with the left, to show how impossible it would have been to make that wound by itself. For another example, a woman   *25* was called to give evidence that the prisoner was a good man. The figure at that time stood on the floor in front of her, looking her full in the face. It pointed to the prisoner's evil face with an outstretched hand.

I had noticed something else about these appearances, too.   *30* While it was clear that the people could not see the figure, they showed signs of feeling very uncomfortable when it was near them. The person who suggested that the man had killed himself, stopped to wipe his forehead several times, and muddled his words. The woman's eyes certainly did follow   *35* the figure's pointing finger, and she looked troubled when she looked at the prisoner's face.

On the eighth day of the trial, after the pause which was made every afternoon for a few minutes rest, I came back into court with the rest of the jury, a little while before the return of the judges. I stood up and looked round. I thought
5 the figure was not there, until I looked to the seats upstairs. There it was, leaning over a woman's shoulder to see if the judges were back or not. Immediately afterwards, that woman screamed, fainted, and was carried out. The same thing happened to one of the judges. When the case was over,
10 and he sat back to read all the evidence, the murdered man entered by the judge's door, came to the judge's desk, and looked eagerly over his shoulder at the pages of notes that he was reading. A change came over the judge's face, his hand stopped, the strange shiver that I knew so well passed over
15 him. He spoke unsteadily, 'Excuse me, gentlemen. I don't feel very well. It must be the air in here.' And he did not recover until he had drunk a glass of water.

The end of the case

Through all those long ten days of the trial, with the same people in the court, the same fog outside, the same rain drip-
20 ping down, the murdered man remained clear in my eyes. I never once saw him look at the prisoner, and again and again I wondered 'Why doesn't he?' But he never did.

And he never looked at me again after the picture was shown, until the closing minutes of the trial arrived. We, the
25 jury, went out to consider our verdict at seven minutes to ten at night. The three members of the jury, whom I mentioned before were not sure that the prisoner was guilty, made a lot of trouble. Nine of us had made our decision, and at last, after going over a few points again, the others agreed with us.
30 We returned to the court at ten past twelve.

The murdered man stood directly opposite the jury-box, on the other side of the court. As I took my place, his eyes rested on me with great attention. He seemed satisfied, and slowly shook a great grey cloth, which he carried for the first

time, over his head and body. As I gave our decision, 'Guilty,'
the cloth fell down, all was gone, and his place was empty.

The murderer was asked by the judge if he had anything to
say before the sentence of death should be passed on him. He
whispered something which was described in the newspapers   5
next day as 'a few senseless words, in which he was heard to
complain that he had not had a fair trial, because the leader
of the jury was against him from the beginning.'

The surprising statement he really made was this:

'My Lord, I knew I was a dead man when the leader of my   10
jury came into the box. My Lord, I knew he would never let
me off, because, before I was taken, he somehow got to my
bedside in the night, woke me, and put a rope round my
neck.'

5 The Signalman

'Hello, below there.'

He heard the voice calling to him. He was standing at the
door of his box. There was a flag in his hand, folded round
its short pole. Surely he knew where the voice came from?
5 But instead of looking up to where I stood at the top of the
steep bank over his head, he turned and looked down the
line. There was something strange in the way he did this,
though I could not have said what.

'Hello, below.'

10 From looking down the line, he turned around again, and,
raising his eyes, saw me high above him.

'Is there a path by which I can come down and speak to
you?' I shouted.

He looked up at me without replying. Just then the earth
15 began to shake, and a rush of air made me jump back. When
the steam from the train had passed, I looked down again.
The man was now re-folding the flag he had shown when the
train went by. I repeated my question. After a short pause,
he pointed with his flag to a spot on the bank about two
20 hundred yards from where I stood. I called 'All right,' and
made my way to that point. I found a rough zig-zag path
leading down. It was very steep and dangerous. It was made
of some wet kind of stone that got wetter as I went down.
When I was half-way down, I looked for the man again. He
25 was standing between the rails on the side where the train
had just passed. He had his left hand at his chin and seemed
lost in thought. I continued down the path, and at last
reached the bottom. As I drew near to the man I saw that he
was very pale, with a dark beard and eye-brows. This place,
30 where he worked, was very lonely and dark. On each side was
a wall of rough stone, which cut out all the view except for
a strip of sky. In one direction the railway lines stretched on

and on between the walls, and in the other, they disappeared
into the great black mouth of a tunnel. There was a red light
just outside the tunnel entrance. The sunlight hardly ever
found its way down here, and there was a nasty, dead smell
all around. It was cold too, for the wind rushed through   5
along the line. I felt that I had left the normal world behind.
  Before the man moved, I was almost near enough to touch
him. He did not take his eyes from my face, but stepped back
one step, and lifted his hand.
  'This is a very lonely place to work,' I said. 'It looked so   10
interesting from where I stood, up on top, that I felt I must
come down and talk to you. I suppose you don't get many
visitors?' He did not reply. Instead, he looked hard at the red
light near the tunnel entrance. He looked all round it, as if
searching for something, then he looked back at me.   15
  'You look after that light, I expect,' I said.
  He answered in a low voice, 'Don't you know what I do?'
  I suddenly felt that this man was not real. He seemed more
like a spirit than a normal human being. The thought made
me step back, and I noticed he was looking at me fearfully.   20
  'You look at me as if you were afraid of me,' I said, trying
to smile.
  'I thought I had seen you before,' he answered.
  'Where?' I asked.
  He pointed to the red light he had looked at.   25
  'There?' I said. 'My good man, what would I be doing
there? However, I never was there, you may believe that.'
  'I think I may,' he said, slowly. 'Yes, I think I may.'
  His manner changed now, and he began to speak quite
freely to me. I asked him many questions, and found out that   30
his work was not hard, but was very important for the safety
of the trains. He had to change the signal, look after the
lights and turn an iron handle now and again. He had spent
many of his lonely hours in learning a foreign language, and
teaching himself mathematics. He had never been much good   35
at learning at school.
  I asked him if he always had to stay down here when he

was on duty. Was he sometimes able to get up into the fresh
air at the top of the steep bank? He replied that, yes, he
sometimes went up to the top, if there were not many trains
due. But he was always having to listen for his electric bell,
5 and didn't like to go too far in case he missed hearing it.

He took me into his box where there was a fire, a desk for
a large book, a telegraphic instrument with a dial and needles,
and the little bell he had just spoken about.

We sat and talked. The little bell rang several times and he
10 had to read off messages and send replies. Once he had to
stand outside the door and show his flag while a train went
by. He seemed to do his job thoroughly and well. Twice,
however, he broke off speaking to me, and with a pale face,
looked at the little bell when it did NOT ring. He then
15 opened the door of the box and looked towards the red light
near the mouth of the tunnel. Both times he came back to
the fire looking rather worried and a little frightened.

When the time came for me to leave, I thanked him and
said, 'You seem to be quite happy, working down here.'
20 'I used to be, sir,' he replied, 'but I am worried, sir, I am
worried.'

'What about?' I asked. 'What is the trouble?'

'It is very difficult to explain, sir. It is very hard to speak
of. If you ever visit me again I will try to tell you.'
25 'But I certainly mean to come and see you again,' I replied.
'When shall I come?'

'I go off early in the morning and I shall be here again at
ten tomorrow night, sir.'

'I will come at eleven.'
30 He thanked me, and we went outside.

'I'll show my white light, sir,' he said in his strange low
voice, 'till you have found the way up. When you have found
it, don't call out. And when you are at the top, don't call
out.'
35 I thought this strange but said, 'Very well.'

'And when you come down tomorrow night, don't call
out. Let me ask you a last question. What made you cry out,

"Hello, below there," tonight?'

'Heaven knows,' I said. 'I cried something like that . . .'

'Not like that, sir. Those were the very words. I know them well.'

'Well, if I said those words, it was, no doubt, because I saw you below.' 5

'For no other reason, sir?'

'What other reason could I possibly have?'

'You don't feel that those words were sent to you in any strange way?' 10

'No.'

He wished me goodnight, and held up his light. I walked back down the line of rails, with the very nasty feeling that there was a train coming behind me, and found the path. It was easier going up than it had been to come down, and I 15 got back to my hotel without any trouble.

My second visit

The next night, I started down the path at exactly eleven o'clock. He was waiting for me at the bottom, with his white light on.

'I have not called out,' I said, when we came close together. 20 'May I speak now?'

'Of course, sir.'

'Good evening, then.'

'Good evening, sir,' he replied, shaking my hand. We walked side by side to his box, entered it, closed the door, 25 and sat down by the fire.

'I have made up my mind to tell you what troubles me,' he said, speaking softly. 'I thought you were someone else yesterday evening. That troubles me.'

'That mistake?' 30

'No. That someone else.'

'Who is it?'

'I don't know.'

'He looks like me?'

'I don't know. I never saw the face. The left arm is across the face, and the right arm is waved. *Violently* waved. This way.'

I watched him, as he waved his arm. It was like someone
5 very *urgently* signalling, 'For God's sake clear the way!'

'One moonlit night,' said the man, 'I was sitting here, when I heard a voice cry, "Hello, below there." I jumped up and looked out of the door. I saw this someone else standing by the red light near the tunnel, waving just like I showed you.
10 The voice seemed rough with shouting, and it cried, "Look out! Look out!" And then again, "Hello, below there! Look out!" I caught up my lamp, turned it on red, and ran towards the figure, calling, "What's wrong? What has happened? Where?" It stood just outside the blackness of the tunnel. I
15 went so close to it that I wondered why it kept its sleeve across its eyes. I ran right up to it, and had my hand stretched out to pull the sleeve away, when it was gone.'

'Into the tunnel?' I asked.

'No. I ran on into the tunnel. I stopped and held my lamp
20 high. There was no one there. I ran out again, feeling very frightened. I looked all around the red light with my own red light, and I went up the iron ladder to the platform at the top. I came down again, and ran back here. I telegraphed both ways, "An alarm has been given. Is anything wrong?"
25 The answer came back, both ways, "All is well." '

I tried to tell him that he must have imagined the figure, and that the cry he had heard must have been made by the wind blowing through the telegraph wires.

'Just listen to it, now,' I said.
30 We sat listening for a while, but he said he knew that sound well, and the cry was not like that at all. Also, he had not finished his story.

It was a terrible shock

'Just six hours after the appearance, a terrible accident happened on the line. Only ten hours later, the dead and wounded were brought through the tunnel over the spot where the figure had stood.'

A horrible shiver went down my back. It was indeed most strange. But he had still more to tell.

'That was just a year ago,' he said, laying his hand on my   5
arm. 'Six or seven months passed, and I had recovered from the surprise and shock, when one morning, at dawn, I looked out of the door towards the red light, and saw that figure again.'

'Did it cry out?' I asked.   10

'No. It was silent.'

'Did it wave its arm?'

'No. It leaned against the post of the light, with both hands in front of its face. Like this.'

Once more I watched as he covered his face. It was an act   15
of sadness. I had seen statues standing like that in the graveyard.

'Did you go up to it?'

'I came in and sat down, because I felt ill. When I went to the door again, it was daylight, and the ghost had gone.'   20

'But did nothing happen after this?'

He touched me on the arm, and nodded.

'That very day, as a train came out of the tunnel, I noticed somebody waving at a carriage window on my side. I saw it just in time to signal the driver to stop. He shut off the   25
engine, and put his brake on, but the train ran on for a hundred yards or more. I ran after it, and as I went along, I heard terrible screams and cries. A beautiful young lady had died suddenly in the train, and was brought in here and laid down on this floor where we are sitting.'   30

I jumped up and looked down at the floor, then up at him.

'It's true, sir. Exactly as it happened.'

I couldn't think of anything to say, and my mouth was very dry.

He continued talking.   35

'Now, sir, listen to this. Then perhaps you will understand why I am so troubled. The ghost came back, a week ago. Ever since, it has been there, now and again.'

'At the light?'

'Yes. At the danger-light.'

'What does it seem to do?'

5   He repeated that first action of the arm waving, as if to
say, 'For God's sake clear the way.'

Then he went on. 'I have no peace or rest. It calls to me
for many minutes together, "Below there! Look out! Look
out!" It stands waving to me. It rings my little bell.'

10   'Did it ring your bell yesterday evening when I was here,
and you went to the door?'

'Twice.'

'Now, look,' I said. 'I was watching the bell, and my ears
were open, and I am quite sure that it did NOT ring at those

15   times. No, nor at any other time, except when it was rung by
someone at the station, trying to get in touch with you.'

He shook his head. 'I have never made a mistake like that,
sir. The ghost's ring is quite different from that of a normal
man. And I have never noticed the bell move, when *he* rings

20   it. I am not surprised that you failed to hear. But *I* heard it.'

'And did the ghost seem to be there when you looked out?'

'It WAS there.'

'Both times?'

He repeated firmly, 'Both times.'

25   'Will you come to the door with me, and look for it now?'

He bit his lower lip, as if unwilling to go outside, but he
got up. I opened the door, and stood on the step, while he
stood in the doorway. There was the danger-light. There was
the great black mouth of the tunnel. There were the high

30   wet stone walls, and there were the stars above them.

'Do you see it?' I asked, looking carefully at his face. His
eyes strained towards the spot.

'No,' he answered. 'It is not there.'

'I agree,' I said.

35   We went in again and shut the door.

'You will understand, sir, that what troubles me so much is
what does the ghost mean? What is it warning against? What

is the danger? Where is the danger? There is danger somewhere on the line. Something terrible will happen, I am sure.
Look at what happened before. But this is very cruel to me.
What can *I* do?'
 He took out his handkerchief and wiped his forehead. *5*
 'If I telegraph "Danger", I can give no reason for it. I should
get into trouble, and do no good. They would think I was
mad. This is the way it would work: Message: "Danger: Take
care." Answer: "What danger? Where?" Message: "Don't
know. But for God's sake take care!" They would dismiss *10*
me. What else could they do?'
 I felt very sorry for him.
 'When it first stood under the danger-light,' he went on,
'why didn't it tell me where the accident was to happen, if it
must happen? Why not tell me how to stop it? When it came *15*
the second time and hid its face, why not tell me "She is
going to die. Let them keep her at home"? If it came on
those two days, only to show me that its warnings were true,
and so prepare me for the third, why not warn me plainly
now? And why me? I'm only a poor signalman. Why not go *20*
to someone more important, who would have power to act?'
 I could not answer him. But I tried to calm him. It was
important that he should try to forget the appearances, and
settle down to do his job properly. The safety of the people
travelling on the trains was in his hands. I offered to stay *25*
with him through the night, but he would not let me. So I
left at two in the morning.
 As I went back up the steep path, I paused once or twice
to look at the red light. I did not like the way those two terrible things had happened, so soon after the appearance of *30*
the ghost. But what should I do? It would be unfair of me to
go and tell his boss about all this. But I knew something
would have to be done, or the man would go mad. I decided
at last to offer to go with him to see a good doctor. We
would see what he thought about this business. The man had *35*
told me that he would be off duty during the next day, but
would start work again just after sunset. I had promised to

go again to see him then.

A sad ending

Next evening was a lovely evening, and I walked out early to enjoy it. The sun was not quite down when I crossed the field towards the railway line. I decided to go for a longer
5 walk, half an hour there, and half an hour back. Then it would be time to go down to the signalman's box.

Before I started off, however, I stepped to the edge of the bank and looked down from the same point where I had first seen him. I cannot describe the terrible feeling that came over
10 me when, close to the tunnel, I saw the appearance of a man, with his left sleeve over his eyes, violently waving his right arm.

The terrible feeling of fear left me, for looking more close-ly, I saw that this was indeed a human being. He seemed
15 to be showing his actions to a group of men who stood nearby. The danger-light was not yet lit. Beside it was a little low hut which I had not seen before. It looked no bigger than a bed.

I knew at once that something was wrong, and blamed myself for leaving the man there alone with no one to look after him and see what he was doing. I went down the zig-zag path as quickly as I could.

5   'What is the matter?' I asked the men.

'A signalman was killed this morning.'

'Not the man belonging to that box?'

'Did you know him, sir? Come and see,' the man replied.

'Oh! How did this happen, how did this happen?' I asked,
10   turning from one to another.

'He was knocked down by an engine, sir. No man in England knew his job better than he did. But somehow he was not clear of the outer rail. It was just at daylight, and he had put out the light. He had his lamp in his hand. As the
15   engine came out of the tunnel he had his back towards it, and it knocked him down. That man drove the engine, and was showing how it happened. Show the gentleman, Tom.'

The engine driver stepped back to his place at the mouth of the tunnel.

20   'As I came round the bend in the tunnel, sir,' he said, 'I saw him at the end. There was no time to stop, and I knew he was a very careful man. He didn't seem to hear the whistle, and I shut it off as we were nearly on top of him. I called to him as loudly as I could.'

25   'What did you say?'

'I said, "Below there! Look out! Look out! For God's sake clear the way!" ' I shivered.

'Ah! It was a terrible time, sir. I never stopped calling to him. I put this arm in front of my eyes, so as not to see, and
30   I waved this arm to the end. But it was no good.'

As I close this strange story, I would just like to point out one thing. It is a fact that the warning that the engine driver gave included not only the words which the poor signalman had repeated to me as haunting him. It also included the
35   words which I had added in my own mind to the actions he had made.

6 The Baron of Grogzwig

The Baron* lived in an old castle in Germany. He came from
a good family, and was quite rich. He was a fine tall man,
with black hair, and a black moustache. He wore a suit made
of the finest green cloth, and red leather boots. He always
had a trumpet hanging from his shoulder, and when he blew   5
it, twenty-four other gentlemen, all dressed in the same
coloured cloth, came to him at once. Then they and the
Baron would go out to hunt the wild pig, or perhaps a bear.
Because of the colour of the clothes they wore, these twenty-
four men were known as the Lincoln Greens. They spent   10
many happy days and nights drinking and eating with the
Baron. It was all great fun.
  But after a while the Baron began to be bored by his
friends. He felt he needed a change from sitting down to
dinner with the same twenty-four men, always talking about   15
the same things, and telling the same stories. He began quar-
relling with them, and tried kicking two or three of them
every night after dinner. This was a pleasant change at first,
but it became boring after a week or so, and the Baron began
to look around for another way in which to amuse himself.   20
  One night, after he and his friends had been out bear
hunting, the Baron sat at the top of his table, looking very
discontented. He swallowed huge glasses of wine, but the
more he swallowed, the more he looked unhappy.
  Suddenly he jumped up.   25
  'I will,' he cried, hitting the table with his hand. 'Gentlemen, fill your glasses, and drink to the Lady of Grogzwig.'
  Twenty-four glasses were raised, and down twenty-four
throats went twenty-four pints of the best white wine.
  'I shall go to the Baron Von Swillenhausen tomorrow and   30
demand that he gives me his daughter in marriage. If he

*baron, a nobleman.

refuses, I will cut off his nose.'

The Baron Von Swillenhausen was lucky that he had a
good and sensible daughter. She did not refuse the Baron of
Grogzwig, and there was much feasting and merry-making.

5   For six weeks, the wild pigs and the bears had a holiday,
and the Baron's trumpet grew rusty from lack of use. The
Lincoln Greens had a wonderful time, eating and drinking,
but sad to say, their happy days were almost at an end.

Changes at Grogzwig Castle

'My dear,' said the Baroness one day.

10   'My love,' said the Baron.

'Those terrible, noisy men.'

'Which, madam?' said the Baron, jumping up.

The Baroness pointed out of the window to where the
Lincoln Greens were having a drink before setting out to

15   hunt a pig or two.

'Those are my huntsmen, madam,' said the Baron.

'Send them away,' whispered the Baroness.

'Send them away!' cried the Baron in surprise.

'To please me, my love,' replied the Baroness.

20   'To please the devil, madam,' answered the Baron.

The Baroness gave a great cry, and fainted at the Baron's
feet.

What could he do? He called for his wife's maid, and sent
for the doctor. Then he rushed into the yard, kicked the two

25   Lincoln Greens who were the most used to it, and gave them
orders to go.

From then on, things went from bad to worse. Day by
day, and year by year, the Baroness changed things in the
castle. So by the time he was a fat fellow of forty-eight, the

30   baron had no feasting, fun, or huntsmen to amuse him.
Instead he had a house full of children. For each year, for
twelve years, the Baroness gave him a son or a daughter. His
wife's family had taken a dislike to him, and he got into debt
and lost nearly all his money.

'I don't see what I can do to make things any better,' said
the Baron to himself. I think I'll kill myself.'

This was a good idea. The Baron took an old hunting knife
from a cupboard nearby, and sharpened it on his boot. Then
he pointed it at his throat.   5

'Hm,' he said, 'perhaps it is not sharp enough.'

He sharpened it again, and had another try, but just at that
moment there was a loud scream from the room upstairs
where his children were playing.

'If I was unmarried,' sighed the Baron, 'I could have done   10
it fifty times by now.'

He called to a servant, and asked for a bottle of wine and a
pipe to be placed in the small room behind the hall. Half an
hour later, the Baron went to the little room. It looked very
comfortable, for there was a log fire burning, and his wine   15
and pipe stood ready on a table.

An unexpected guest

'Leave the lamp,' said the Baron to his servant.

'Anything else, my lord?' asked the servant.

'No, thank you. You may go.'

The servant left the room, and the Baron locked the door.   20

'I'll smoke a last pipe,' said the Baron, 'then I'll be off.'

So, putting the knife on the table till he wanted it, the
Baron filled his glass with the wine, and sat down to enjoy his
last pipe.

He thought about a great many things. About his present   25
troubles and past days of happiness. He thought about the
Lincoln Greens who were all in different parts of the country. He was thinking of wild pigs and bears, when he raised
his eyes and found to his great surprise, that he was not
alone.   30

No, he was not, for, on the opposite side of the fire someone else was sitting. It was a terrible figure, with deep red
eyes, and a very long, thin face. He had thick black hair. His

coat was blue, and fastened down the front with coffin*
handles. He had coffin plates on his legs, like armour. He
took no notice of the Baron, but sat looking into the fire.

    'Hello!' said the Baron, loudly, and stamped his foot to
5 get his attention.

    'Hello!' replied the stranger, moving his eyes towards the
Baron, but not his face or himself. 'What now?'

    'What now!' replied the Baron. '*I* should ask that question.
How did you get in here?'

10   'Through the door,' replied the figure.

    'What are you?' asked the Baron.

    'A man,' replied the figure.

    'I don't believe it,' said the Baron.

    'Don't then,' said the figure.

15   'I won't,' said the Baron.

    The figure looked at the Baron for some time, then said, 'I
see I can't fool you. I'm not a man.'

    'What are you then?' asked the Baron.

    'I am the Ghost of Despair and Suicide,' said the figure. As
20 he spoke, he turned towards the Baron. The Baron could see
that he had a long piece of wood running through the centre
of his body. The figure pulled this out, and laid it on the
table, with no more fuss than if it had been a walking stick.

    'Now,' said the figure, looking over to the hunting knife,
25 'are you ready for me?'

    'Not quite,' replied the Baron. 'I must finish this pipe
first.'

    'Be quick, then,' said the figure.

    'You seem in a hurry,' said the Baron.

30   'Why, yes, I am,' answered the figure. 'There's lots of
people waiting for me all over England and France at the
moment, and I am very busy.'

    'Do you drink?' said the Baron, touching the bottle with
the end of his pipe.

35   'Nine times out of ten, and then very hard,' said the figure.

*coffin, box in which a dead person is buried.

Why should I do it?

The Baron took another good look at his new friend. He was certainly a very strange person. At last, he asked him if he ever took an active part in the act he was thinking of carrying out.

5   'No,' said the figure, 'but I am always there.'

'Just to see fair play, I suppose?' said the Baron.

'Just that,' said the figure. 'Be as quick as you can, will you. There is a young gentleman who has too much money and too much time to waste, waiting for me now.'

10   'Going to kill himself because he's got too much money,' said the Baron, quite amused. 'Ha! ha! that's a good one.' (This was the first time that the Baron had laughed for a very long time).

'I say,' cried the figure, looking very frightened, 'don't do

15   that again.'

'Why not?' demanded the Baron.

'Because it gives me pain all over,' replied the figure. 'Sigh as much as you like, that does me good.'

The Baron sighed without thinking, at the mention of the

20   word, and the figure looked better. It took the hunting knife and handed it to the Baron.

'It's not a bad idea though,' said the Baron, feeling the edge of the knife. 'A man killing himself because he has too much money.'

25   'Pooh!' said the ghost, 'no better than a man's killing himself because he has none or little.'

Whether the ghost knew what he was saying, or whether he thought that the Baron's mind was so made up that nothing would change it, I don't know. I only know that the Baron

30   stopped his hand, all of a sudden, opened his eyes wide, and looked as if new life had come into him for the very first time.

'Why, of course,' he said, 'nothing is so bad that it can't be made better again.'

35   'Except an empty purse,' said the ghost.

'Well, but it may one day be filled again,' said the Baron.

'Scolding wives,' cried the ghost.

'Oh, they may be quietened,' said the Baron.

'Twelve children,' shouted the ghost.

'Can't all go wrong, surely,' said the Baron.   5

The ghost was getting very angry with the Baron, and told him that when he had finished joking, he would be happy if he got on with killing himself.

'But I am not joking,' said the Baron.

'Then hurry up,' said the ghost. 'Leave this terrible life at   10
once.'

'I don't know,' said the Baron, playing with the knife. 'It's not a very happy one certainly, but I'm not sure that yours is any better. How do I know that I shall be any better off when I have left this world?'   15

'Hurry up!' screamed the ghost.

'Keep away!' said the Baron. 'I'm not going to feel sorry for myself any more. I shall go and speak to the Baroness first. Then I'll try the fresh air and the bears again.' He fell back into his chair, laughing.   20

The figure went back a step or two, looking at the Baron with great fear. When the laughing stopped, the ghost caught up the piece of wood, pushed it hard into its body, gave a terrible scream, and disappeared.

The Baron never saw it again. He made up his mind to give   25
life another try, and soon had the Baroness and her family doing what he wanted. He died many years later, not a rich man, but certainly a very happy one.

Questions

Black Coll and the Devil's Inn

1. Why did no one like Black Coll?
2. Where did Black Coll first meet Colonel Blake?
3. Why was Evleen so afraid of Black Coll?
4. How does a burrag-bos work?
5. What did Black Coll do with the burrag-bos when he got it?
6. How did Pexie manage to get Evleen up to the Devil's Inn?
7. What happened to Evleen when she woke up?

Two Boxes of Gold

1. What started Mr Blamyre's adventures?
2. Why did Mr Blamyre pretend to be a travelling salesman?
3. Tell in your own words, the dream Mr Blamyre had on the train.
4. How did the Major come to be on the same train?
5. Something unusual was seen near the station. What was it?
6. When they reached Marseilles, where did Mr Levison take his friends for the night, and what was the place like?
7. What was in the telegram from London. Was it good news, or bad?

George and Geoffrey

1. How did George and Susan meet?
2. Why did the Archer family want Susan to marry Gibbs, and why was she so against it?
3. In her letter, what did Susan ask George to do?
4. What had the villagers heard about Gibbs and his wife?
5. Why was Susan so afraid that her son might be killed?
6. Did George admit to doing the murder?
7. What were the points against George?
8. What was the happy ending to the story?

A Ghost Story

1. What strange thing happened when I read about the scene of the murder in the newspaper?
2. What did I notice about the two men walking down the street?
3. Who did I see coming out of my dressing-room one night?
4. What did the ghost do when the jury was shown a picture of the murdered man?
5. How did people behave when the ghost stood close to them?
6. What did the ghost do after the verdict was given?
7. Why did the prisoner feel that the foreman of the jury was against him from the beginning of the trial?

The Signalman

1. What did the signalman do when he first heard me calling to him?
2. Describe in your own words, what it was like, down near the railway line.
3. What did the figure cry out to the signalman?
4. Was there really someone there?
5. What happened six hours after the first appearance of the ghost?
6. After the second time the ghost appeared, what happened?
7. How was the signalman killed?

The Baron of Grogzwig

1. Why were the Lincoln Greens sent away?
2. What happened to the Baron and his family in the next twelve years?
3. What did the Baron intend to do before he killed himself?
4. Describe the unexpected guest.
5. Something the ghost said made the Baron laugh. What was it?
6. Why didn't the ghost like laughter?
7. What changed the Baron's mind about taking his own life?

Oxford Progressive English Readers

Introductory Grade

Vocabulary restricted to 1400 headwords
Illustrated in full colour

Grade 1

Vocabulary restricted to 2100 headwords
Illustrated in full colour

Grade 2

Vocabulary restricted to 3100 headwords
Illustrated in colour

Grade 2 (cont.)

The Hound of the Baskervilles	Sir Arthur Conan Doyle
The Missing Scientist	S.F. Stevens
The Red Badge of Courage	Stephen Crane
Robinson Crusoe	Daniel Defoe
Seven Chinese Stories	T.J. Sheridan
Stories of Shakespeare's Plays 2	Retold by Wyatt & Fullerton
A Tale of Two Cities	Charles Dickens
Tales of Crime and Detection	Retold by G.F. Wear
Two Boxes of Gold and Other Stories	Charles Dickens

Grade 3

Vocabulary restricted to 3700 headwords
Illustrated in colour

Battle of Wits at Crimson Cliff	Retold by Benjamin Chia
Dr Jekyll and Mr Hyde and Other Stories	R.L. Stevenson
From Russia, with Love	Ian Fleming
The Gifts and Other Stories	O. Henry & Others
The Good Earth	Pearl S. Buck
Journey to the Centre of the Earth	Jules Verne
Kidnapped	R.L. Stevenson
King Solomon's Mines	H. Rider Haggard
Lady Precious Stream	S.I. Hsiung
The Light of Day	Eric Ambler
Moonraker	Ian Fleming
The Moonstone	Wilkie Collins
A Night of Terror and Other Strange Tales	Guy De Maupassant
Seven Stories	H.G. Wells
Stories of Shakespeare's Plays 3	Retold by H.G. Wyatt
Tales of Mystery and Imagination	Edgar Allan Poe
20,000 Leagues Under the Sea	Jules Verne
The War of the Worlds	H.G. Wells
The Woman in White	Wilkie Collins
Wuthering Heights	Emily Brontë
You Only Live Twice	Ian Fleming

Grade 4

Vocabulary within a 5000 headwords range
Illustrated in black and white

The Diamond as Big as the Ritz and Other Stories	F. Scott Fitzgerald
Dragon Seed	Pearl S. Buck
Frankenstein	Mary Shelley
The Mayor of Casterbridge	Thomas Hardy
Pride and Prejudice	Jane Austen
The Stalled Ox and Other Stories	Saki
The Thimble and Other Stories	D.H. Lawrence